Copy Cookbook : Making Buffalo Wild Wings Most Popular Recipes at Home

Disclaimer

Contents

Use duplicate recipes from restaurants and save more than

Copycat books

Do you have a favorite restaurant? What about your favorite food you want to eat in the restaurant? When I ask people, they seem to do a lot of things - though it's also true that many of us have more than one pet. Some people like baby's spine, fajitas, paella, dishes or steaks, while others eat burgers, fried chicken or pizza, but whichever you prefer, I'm sure you'll prefer it if you're ready as you like .

Of course, we don't eat our favorite restaurant every day. In fact, we don't eat every night - it's not practical, especially if you have a family and you don't talk about money, then you certainly can't afford it. However, you can consider some of your favorite dishes in the restaurant for a homemade menu. This may sound like a pipe dream, but it can be much easier than you think.

The key to preparing food in a restaurant in the home knows how to prepare it, as well as a list of special ingredients needed - that is, recipes. As you might expect, the recipe used by large restaurants is unknown and, in many cases, hidden secrets. While you may not find the right recipe used by large restaurants, some smart chefs have found ways to make recipes that are similar to restaurant favorites. With the help of "coffee recipe books" made by these chefs, you can animate your home menu and cook your own dishes in restaurants where you can't go to restaurants.

Copycat the named cook

Have you ever wondered if you can prepare food and food at

home? I hope many do. It's not that he doesn't want to go to a restaurant; sometimes you just have to eat at home and you want to make your favorite restaurant dishes in your kitchen. This is certainly true if you have a young family and cannot go to restaurants as often as you like, but the same can happen if your family budget is limited and is not extended to several nights, or if you prefer . Selling chain restaurants from home is not easy.

Of course, avant-garde restaurants usually don't advertise the right recipes. Why, like ordinary restaurants, should be the biggest draw for customers. In fact, in many cases, restaurants are not afraid to tell the public that their popular sauces, spices, or dishes are made from secret recipes.

Copying a recipe book is probably the best answer. This is a cookbook showcasing independently developed recipes for restaurant tastings. Of course, the recipe isn't a true restaurant recipe, so it's not an original copy of the original, but that doesn't mean you and your family don't care. Until you try, you don't know, but if you try this kind of food, you can make food at home!

Copy Prescription - Do something special

Copycat restaurant recipes, often called secret recipes, have revolutionized the local community. The recent inclusion of recipes has made cooking more enjoyable for me. I like to cook but I like to cook things in the restaurant. It's fun when the food is good or better than your favorite restaurant.

The recipes at Copycat Restaurant offer a variety of options for cooking dinner. My wife and I often like to go to Chile, but lately there are some things we love to cook. The solution ... does it yourself. That's true many chili recipes in most textbooks are copyrighted. It is very simple as long as you have the recipe.

We loved the chili roll and boneless wings salad in Shanghai, but we stopped. We also like PF Chang, Mongolian Beef, but PF Chang is not where we live. These recipes are also available.

We love to make alfresco from Olive Garden, chicken macaroni from Macaroni Grill, and many of our other favorite dishes from elsewhere. Alfredo is very simple. In fact, this is one of the easiest things you can do.

The recipes at Copycat restaurants allow you to manage food using only a fraction of the price of restaurant food. If you want to cut costs, cooking food in a restaurant can save you a lot of money. Alfred's pasta flour costs only four or three dollars for three or four dollars, not thirty dollars or more at a restaurant.

Copycat recipes and restaurant cuisine are similar. He was surprised by the results.

Quick Copy - Copy Your Favorite Edits

Learn feelings, an irresistible urge to let go of everything you do and get your favorite fast food. You may be amazed while watching TV and ads pop up with loving images or videos from hot thieves, Taco, chicken or French fries, back to the remote camp and now he wants his favorite burger, see the billboard for this taco and now he has to. The worst times are when you feel good at home and you don't want to leave, but that desire is great ... it can happen anywhere and anytime.

How often do you like to copy your favorite fast food recipes or restaurants at home with copies of fast food? He screamed and thought about the wonderful tasting offer offered by his favorite restaurant that they really like? An integrated view of a secret kitchen hidden underground with doctoral students making menu items that cannot be seen by the audience, or the CEO of a company that joins six armed guards to dismantle the Fort Knox type for a recipe that has opened a world-famous reputation for the world.

While it might be good to cook a copy of your favorite fast food at home, you also know that original recipes are unhealthy in many ways, high in salt and fat, even though you may be that they will not suit your taste and your stomach, but you know that it must mimic the unhealthy things that make up your heart and kidneys but still maintain your extraordinary taste and satisfaction.

You also know that copying your favorite menu settings can save you from friends and family and save many copies at home. .

I know I often make "secret" recipes for McDonald's Big Macs and special sauces, King Burger burgers, KFC Original or even Starbucks milk, we may say, but these are just one word: "secrets."

Whether it's computer hardware and software to cars - you can redesign things to make almost perfect replicas of food; repeat the fast food restaurant, don't really know the original recipe, or break into the basement, or install a spy camera in McDonald's kitchen, or even kidnap the CEO and store it as a ransom for the food he needs.

With this reverse design recipe, you can easily make your home the way you want, anytime, anywhere, and use a healthier alternative to the salt and fat used by older boys. All you have to do is search for a copy of a fast food recipe book during your stay and find the right way to create personal and famous menu items at any time, day or night.

So stop craving and start making your favorite restaurant menu items by following the instructions in the cookbook, which everyone can read and prepare after you forgive the cookbook.

Copycat recipe reviews

Copycat's cookbook features a number of popular restaurant recipes that offer thousands of recipes for hundreds of restaurants in the United States, from fast food to high-quality guests. The recipe is carefully prepared by a chef who has been cooking for years. But I have learned on my own that this is not very difficult to do if they have the exact instructions and the necessary content!

One of my favorite things is cooking in one of my girlfriend's favorite restaurants for the comfort of my home. He didn't know how to make it, and I'll never tell him my secret that it's a recipe book with all those recipes; I'll just make you think I'm a great cook!

It is also surprising how cheaper it is to cook very spicy food from your home. You might think that most of the $ 50- $ 60 restaurants served in restaurants will cost at least $ 20 if they come together, but most are only a few dollars. This made me realize how many of these restaurants make money.

Some of my favorite restaurants that I often cook from the kitchen are Red Lobster, Macaroni Grill, Cracker Barrel, Outback Steakhouse and my favorite, Olive Garden.

Getting recipes from your favorite restaurant is a great idea if you want to cook and save money.

Some reasons why I really like recipe books:

1) I also love to cook for myself and my relatives.

2) Save a lot of money.

3) People now think I'm an excellent cook.

4) I usually prefer a plate for meetings (but I keep my food a secret resolution)

5) I can eat my favorite food on a bigger budget because it doesn't cost much more.

But obviously good news is always missing.

Some obvious reasons why this isn't for everyone:

1) Food can contain many ingredients that can cause

problems.

2) What you cook at home needs to be cleaned up when finished.

3) You don't have to have someone waiting for you.

Do you make a copy of the recipe or do you like to eat it?

Most of us love to eat in restaurants. We see in the secret of the recipes of their restaurants that there is no way to do it at home.

It's a secret cook, right? Going out to dinner, having a casual dinner with your family, someone who lives with you and who cleans up, great things, what could be better? Well, it's all amazing, but the price of a casual dinner can change at night.

I went to dinner with my family last weekend. We enjoyed our dinner and everything was excellent. It was an unusual moment, that is, until we received the invoice. That adds $ 100 to $ 100 if I add it to the top. Meals cost $ 100 for five families, it's worth buying a two-week shop or two-week gasoline for my two cars. When bills are paid, I feel bad in my stomach. It's fun to enjoy the luxury of life, but spending $ 100 to get out isn't at the top of the to-do list.

And if I say, can you make the same restaurant recipe as you do at home? You may not think the quality and taste is the same as what you get when you eat, but you can. Obviously, the only downside to the kitchen is that there is no server, bus or dishwasher, but it saves you $ 100, which is worth it.

Find copies of your favorite recipes, restaurant recipes or chain recipes and you're sure to find plenty of information. I also discovered that some of my favorite American restaurants actually offer secret recipes on their site.

There are many cookbooks you can buy that reveal the recipes for the perfect restaurant you need. Of course, this recipe book isn't exactly the recipe, but it's made by a cook, who spends hours trying and tasting it until it tastes right.

Prescription conventions and blogs, as well as the online recipe community, are great ways to get copy recipes. You can also get a lot of information from the people who read and tested it and who learn about their results and mistakes. Sometimes you need special kitchen equipment that goes beyond simple cookware, but many recipes are easy to follow. I saw someone ask me what it was and then I tried it and I was surprised at how tasty the restaurant was, which I thought was really good.

So I want to encourage the recipes of restaurants that create nostalgia, I do it too and I only deal with the fact that I only need my dishwasher.

Use duplicate recipes from restaurants and save more than money

Let's face it; most of us today don't have much time in the kitchen. There is always work to be done, monuments and attractions and time does not work. Exclusion or a visit to the restaurant carefully solves the problem, right? This may seem like a short-term solution, but as a long-term solution, the nose can damage the face. If you can make a copy of your restaurant recipe and cook it at home, you can save money and more without losing the good things in life. Going to a restaurant and taking it is expensive, not only in the hip pocket, but in the waist as well. It tastes good, but you can't control what goes into the food. You don't really know what you're eating. Some restaurants provide information on the nutritional value of your meal, but this is not yours. The problem is that the food often tastes better and sometimes they just want a restaurant. It's not just convenience, it's the whole package.

Have you ever sat at home with three different restaurant membranes in your hand and wondered what you want to eat and can't decide? In fact, it will be fun to go to each place and choose the right one. This is impossible compromise. Better than nothing.

What if I could cook at home? You can do this and for a fraction of the cost of a meal. The time factor is present. Why worry about cooking at home if it lasts longer? The reality is that it doesn't last long. The impression that if you have to watch, you actually see how long it takes to cook the ribs or go to a restaurant to eat ribs will be surprising. This, of course, depends on the recipe, but cooking the ribs doesn't take long and the kitchen doesn't spend much time. If you are at home, you can upgrade to another item, which is an extra bonus.

If restaurant food is your business, you can prepare it at home. There are currently cookbooks on the market that have been printed typical restaurant chain dishes They can really do it with groceries and it feels like a real business, so if you like dishes from three different restaurants you could make them at home. "America's Most Wanted Recipe" is an example of a product available on the market and the best of both I've tried. Ron Douglas wrote legible cookbooks, with clear instructions on how to make dishes, and the four or five recipes I tested were the same as the original ones. The other is "Copy Cat Cookbook" which is not very good but worth seeing. So do this and the books are there if you want to try it out.

If you want to save time and money, try cooking your favorite recipes at home. This way you can manage your ingredients and budget at the same time without reducing your taste.

Secrets of Copycat recipe

Many restaurants are internationally renowned for their original recipes. Here is an Italian restaurant that is famous for its pasta dishes in New York, fish and chips, famous American restaurants, Japanese Shabu Shabu restaurants, famous Chinese dumpling restaurants and especially traditional Karekare Filipino German restaurants and so on.

As we know, the restaurant industry is one of our most successful industries of our generation today. Many entrepreneurs want to make their restaurant profitable and have the opportunity to do so. Some newly established restaurant owners mimic recipes from many of the best restaurants in the world.

18

These recipes are called "Secret Copy Recipes". The word scenario means that other words or behaviors are copied; copy, copy or copy.

There are many cookbooks in the bookstore that can be purchased at any time; Some cooking programs are broadcast on TV and millions of recipes can be seen on many websites. These are some of the sources on which they mimic recipes and can make their descriptions secret.

Examples of Copycat's secret recipes

Classic fish and chips:

Ingredients:
- 4 large potatoes, peeled and cut
- 1 cup flour
- 1 teaspoon of aroma
- 1 teaspoon of salt
- 1 teaspoon black pepper
- 1 glass of milk
- 1 egg
- 1 liter of vegetable oil for frying
- 1 kg of cream fillets

Direction
1. Put the potatoes in a medium bowl in cold water. Mix the flour, baking powder, salt and pepper separately in a medium bowl. Mix with milk and eggs; stir until the mixture is smooth. Leave the dough for 20 minutes.

2. Coat the oil at 175 ° F in a large or electric pan.

3. Fry the potatoes in hot oil until soft. Touch them to the handkerchief.

4. Dip the fish one by one in each dish and add boiling oil. Fry until the fish is golden brown. If necessary, raise the temperature to maintain 175 degrees (175 degrees). Also touch a paper napkin.

5. Rub the potatoes again for 1-2 minutes to make them fresh.

This delicious and simple recipe is a favorite dish of New England, referred to as the famous international American restaurant.

The extra ingredients from the original recipe are added to make it tastier and are called fish and chips in New York, served with lemon or sour sauce. This is one of the secret recipes of most international restaurants in America

Things You Must Know Before Eating Wild Buffalo Wings

Everyone knows that watching sports is the most exponential when wings and beer are included and Buffalo Wild Wings is a place where various amusements come together. He found it very difficult to find a place with a flavor other than wing sauces and looked on many televisions that activated all the sports that could be enough to make an adult cry. For this reason, every sports fan who deserves his salt has sometimes spent in this chain and rejuvenating his staff, but it is certainly worth reading how the B-Dub arrive before breaking orders: lost wings.

His real name is Buffalo Wild Wings & Wick.

The founders served their distinctive wings with another Buffalo Area favorite, beef neck. The sandwich consists of hot beef fried in a kummelweck roll, compressed with halal salt and cumin seeds. While New Yorkers like heights, chicken wings are becoming more popular and sandwiches are taken from menus and restaurant names. Now widely known as B-Dubs for February, it is a registered trademark!

Side-by-side bonds are a start of money.

Unsurprisingly, the menu is the most popular chicken wings! The chain sells nearly 2 billion wings per year - over 1 billion wings without bonuses and sells on average 768 million traditional wings or 27 million wings per week. It is estimated that over 100 million were sold in March 2015.

Buffalo Wild Wings creates the taco biz.

King Wing chose to be randomly immersed in one, and in the spring of 2016 he acquired the majority of the R Taco chain (formerly Rusty Taco), serving street tacos, beer and cheap margins.

They have laboratory salt.

There are 21 special sauces, from sweet and tasty BBQ to blazing, which is very much to be feared. B-Dub Salt Sauce is constantly developing new flavors to make customers laugh at hand and regularly let go of their retirement feelings like Wicked Wasabi and Ghost Pepper Manager of Shady

Summer and Sriracha Strawberry.

You can take part in the Blazing Wings Challenge.

Shoppers who love the warmth can sample their taste by consuming the restaurant's 12 hottest wings in less than 6 minutes. Remember to follow the rules: No drinking, no sauce, no vomiting and no mourning.

Classic Buffalo wings

Leave the fried wings in the pub. The steak is dirty and included, and you don't need it when the game is turned on. It is much easier to cook chicken. Give yourself plenty of time. Depending on the size of the wings, they should be kept in the oven for 50-60 minutes before being pickled. In a crispy state, they are thrown into the buffalo and placed in the oven under the grill until they are caramelized.

First the sauce

What is the value of Buffalo Lice? In most cases, it is a simple blend of melted butter and strong sauce. Us? We also want to add honey. For yourself, cook the honey and spicy sauce in a small pan and then shake with butter. Cook until the butter has melted and the sauce is slightly reduced.

Mumps is the key

The key to perfect sharpness is to attach the wings to the wire in the flange furnace. The stem allows air to flow under the wing and allows it to cook evenly.

Feed the masses

This recipe feeds four hungry people. If it's part of a bigger game day, maybe six people will go into it. But there is no harm in multiplying recipes - people always want more Buffalo wings. See the table below to find out how much you should buy!

The ingredients

- 2 pounds of chicken wings
- 2 tablespoons. vegetable oil
- 1 tsp. hvítlauksduft
- Halal salt
- Fresh ground black pepper
- 1/4 c. spicy sauce (like Frank)
- 2 tablespoons. honey
- 4 tablespoons. butter
- costumes to fit
- Carrot characters to serve
- Celery to serve

Travel plans

Preheat the oven to 400 ° and place the wire holder on the baking sheet. Remove the chicken wings with a large bowl of oil and season with garlic powder, salt and pepper. Move to a prefabricated baking dish.

Bake until the chicken is golden and the skin flakes, 50 to 60 minutes, and the wings are half-flat.

In a small skillet, mix hot sauce and honey. Bring to the boil and stir in the butter. Cook until the butter has melted and reduced slightly, approx. Heat silica oil at low temperature for 2 minutes. Add the fried wings to the bowl and stir with the buffalo sauce until completely curled. Return to the wings to tie hands and kick - watch out! to caramel sauce for 3 minutes. Serve with artichoke sauce and vegetables.

The best recipe for Buffalo copycat Wild Wings

They have an unexpected number of immersion options so everyone can get the poultry basket they need. Choose from the traditional delicious flavors of buffalo or the spicy Blazing sauce that melts on your face, or try something else with the Asian Zing sauce or the delicious parmesan sauce. Whether they taste good, they are hot, fresh and dressed with the perfect amount of sauce.

But what if you want to strengthen your hot arm without going to a bar and spending a lot of money on apps and drinks? Can you make your favorite Buffalo Wild Wings recipe at home? You bet you can! Although you can buy the sauce online or on the spot (sometimes you can see it based on cost), it's easy to sign the medium to make the sauce at home. You can even adjust the level of spices if you are such a crazy person that you can treat peppers.

Collect your ingredients to make a copy of the Buffalo Wild Wings recipe

The first step in making recipes for Wings Build Buffalo copies is to learn about the ingredients used in real foods.

Fortunately, this recipe is quite simple because the company sells poultry sauce on Amazon, and we can see a list of ingredients on the label. All we have to do is play around the amount until we feel good.

The list of ingredients starts with vinegar, cayenne pepper, oil, xanthenes gum, spices, garlic and natural and artificial flavor. Almost all the ingredients are found in a bottle of Buffalo Hot Buffalo Sauce, so we use it as a base for our Buffalo Wild Wings sauce. From now on, add more garlic powder, sugar and peppercorns, just like the average Buffalo Wild Wings sauce.

Add corn flour and eggs to thicken, and then sprinkle with Worcestershire sauce to add other ingredients to the list (onions, sugar syrup and rabbits).

For a complete list of ingredients and step-by-step instructions

Do you make bread with Buffalo Wild Wings chicken wings?

We were wondering if we should make a copy of Buffalo Wild Wings with or without a bullet. Chicken wings usually do not contain bread, this is one of the mistakes everyone makes while making Buffalo wings. The skin itself is perfectly connected, so it's not absolutely necessary, but here we go for the sake of originality. We dig and research. It didn't take long for us to agree with our approach: there was no purpose. We got some pieces from employees to Reedit to make sure they didn't reach the bones. The wings are shown only for example. After melting, each worker is forced to

25

throw the current conditions in the oven.

Innocent wings have a difficult path. They're packed and frozen, so we're not 100% sure what happened. The only thing we know for sure is that it contains gluten and wheat (according to an allergy on the Buffalo Wild Wings website) but not bone marrow.

Are Buffalo Wild wings fried or roasted?

Over the years we have heard from both sides of the mature debate about the layers of fried buffalo. Supporters say this is the only way to ensure fresh skin, which is an important ingredient in good warm arms. Grid-side fighters claim that the wings can split very well if roasted in an oven at high temperatures. A lot of oil saves the oven and makes your arms healthier.

We're not here to change our minds when we get to one side or the other, but we wanted to create the most reliable recipe for Wings Wild Buffalo. It turns out the restaurant has hit his wings. Allergic guides on their website confirm that traditional (rejuvenated) and non-rinsing arms are fried when cutting beef, also known as tulip. We had trouble finding fat for our families, so we decided to use high-temperature neutral cooking oil (like rapeseed oil or avocado).

Yes, the Buffalo Wild Wings copy recipe contains eggs

So it may sound like a weird ingredient when it's in sauce, but it's actually a secret ingredient in the Buffalo Wild Wings transcription recipe. This is not one of the ingredients we are calculating. We know that Buffalo Wild Wings sauce contains eggs as they are included in the list of ingredients in their bottled product and include allergen.

What makes eggs so important? Thick sauce until it forms a perfect layer for each dough. Not only that, but the brine also tastes great and tastes rich in sauce. If we look at it from the point of view of food science, then it makes sense. Eggs in spices such as salad dressing and mayonnaise are essential ingredients as their egg yolks can create an emulsion. You see, oil and vinegar do not melt naturally, but the egg provides stability that keeps all the ingredients suspended. Add a little wheat grass to strengthen the structure created with the eggs to create completely dense dough.

Share your wings to create a recipe for Wings Wild Buffalo

Well now that we've covered all the key ingredients, cooking time. We started with chicken wings. You can find different ways to buy wings in supermarkets, where each chicken wings has three parts: wingspan, middle (flat) and softer part (called daulet). Wings are sometimes sold as so-called "party wings" where goods are separated. In other cases, they are sold as whole units.

If you have already purchased a special wing, you can move on to the next step. Alternatively, read the flat wing tips with kitchen scissors or a sharp knife. This section contains almost no meat, so you can throw away or store tips in the fridge to make chicken or bone soup later. Then separate the plane and matrix to get two parts. Sprinkle with white salt over salt and pepper and set aside while making poultry sauce.

27

Make a sauce for this copy of Buffalo Wild Wings

It's time to break free and move on. Get a small skillet and make it with a new chicken-supporting sauce. We start by adding almost everything to the sauce - Red's Frank, cooking oil, ground sugar, garlic powder, and black pepper, cayenne pepper and Worcestershire sauce bubbly the mixture just before evaporating the heat.

Then shake the water and corn in a small bowl to form a precipitate. You can try cereal directly with the sauce, but water it first to prevent unwanted lumps. When the cereal is thinned in the pan, cook for 2 minutes. Stir this mixture for five minutes until it is good and thick. Turn off the heat and let cool for about ten minutes.

Finally it's time to add the eggs. Instead of putting the eggs directly into the sauce, slowly add the egg sauce to pour these oils into the yolk. Finally, you get a nice thick sauce that tastes absolutely amazing.

Prepare the cookie for a recipe for the copy of Buffalo Wild Wings

Once the sauce is over, it's time to fry the wings. While we know that the authentic way to cook Buffalo Wild Wings is beef, we have also found it difficult to find this product in the grocery store. Instead, we used aviation oil in the tests and thought that our wings were perfectly in place. If you have beef, then go! Any other neutral cooking oil can also be used at high temperatures, such as avocado oil or vegetable oil.

Heat about three inches of oil in a large Dutch oven or wok. You can also use the electric oven if you are lucky. Heat the oil to 350 degrees Fahrenheit with a frying thermometer to check the temperature. When the oil reaches the nominal temperature, reduce the heat to a medium-low level to avoid boiling. We don't want chicken wings to burn from the outside before they have been cooked.

Cook your wings to create the perfect recipe for the copy of Buffalo Wild Wings

When the oil is fine and hot, gently release the wings into the oil. If you are concerned with modeling the syringe, gently lower it into the spider pot. Depending on the size of the Dutch oven or electric oven, it may be possible to install all 24 wings simultaneously. Our pots increased by 12, so we cooked them in two batches to prevent the pan from clogging and the oil from overflowing.

Cook the wings for about 10 to 12 minutes until they turn golden yellow and cook at an internal temperature of 165 degrees Fahrenheit. When the wings are done, remove them from the sheets coated with absorbent paper to allow excess oil to leak out. If you have more wings to fry, let the oil turn back 350 degrees before adding more wings. Eat fried wings in the form of a snack while waiting or keep warm in a 200 degree oven. Do not throw them in the sauce until you are ready to eat, otherwise it will be dirty.

Insert the Buffalo Wild Wings script into the script sauce

Be prepared, because this step can be a little messy: everything will be random. The saline part is not entirely scientific. The editors told us that the Buffalo Wild Wings sauce came in a gallon bag equipped with a pump. All six bony wings and eight wings were obtained. Since we don't have a pump at home, we need to measure the right amount of sauce.

After adding the sauce to the wings, mix immediately with a few tabs until they are well covered. If you think this method is too futile, try placing the wings and sauce in a large, airtight container. Shake vigorously until the ingredients are properly coated. Remove the wings from the plate and serve immediately. He may have left the sauce, which was delicious in the fridge for about a week.

How close are we to the original Buffalo Wild Wings recipe?

If boring crowds and expensive beer aren't your choice, here's the recipe. Honestly, we can't tell the difference between our Buffalo Wild Wings recipe and the original recipe.

The sauce contains excellent garlic and spices, which is perfectly suited to the sauce in a restaurant. The wings were perfectly cooked - crispy on the outside and dripping on the inside - and ideally the sauce was thick to create a beautiful layer.

If it's not your favorite sauce, don't worry: you can modify this recipe to prepare another Buffalo Wing sauce. It's as simple as adding an extra cayenne to turn a medium sauce into a spicy sauce or adding garlic pepper and cayenne to a spicy garlic sauce. If you really want to go crazy, add fresh habaneras, jalapeno and maybe pepper to prepare the Blazing sauce. Prepare yourself because these things don't bother you!

- Buffalo Wild Wings Buffalo recipe
- Preparation time: 25 minutes
- Cooking time: 10-12 minutes
- Dose: create 24 wings

Ingredients:

- 1 cup of spicy red buffalo mozzarella sauce
- 1/3 cup of neutral cooking oil (similar to avocado oil)
- 1 teaspoon of sugar
- 1 teaspoon of garlic powder
- 1/2 teaspoon minced black pepper
- 1/2 teaspoon hot pepper
- 1/2 teaspoon Worcestershire sauce
- 2 teaspoons of water
- 2 teaspoons of cornmeal
- 1 egg yolk
- Halal salt to taste
- 2 dozen chicken wings
- Passive cooking oil, such as avocado oil or rapeseed oil

Direction:

In a pan, mix Frank Hot Red cooking oil, granulated sugar, powdered garlic, black pepper, cayenne pepper and Worcestershire sauce. Bring to a boil over medium-high heat until boiling, approx. 5 minutes reduce the heat for cooking.

Mix the flour and corn in a small bowl. Add the contents to the bowl and simmer for 5 minutes until it is thick.

Remove from pan and allow to cool for approx. for 10 minutes.

After the sauce has cooled, place the egg yolks in a medium-sized bowl. Slowly add the cold sauce to your egg yolk with a continuous liquid, frothing constantly while adding to create an emulsion that prevents the oil from separating. When all the sauce has entered the bowl, cover the bowl.

If you prepare the wings immediately, keep the sauce at room temperature until use. Store the sauce in the refrigerator to store the sauce for more than an hour. Remove the poultry from the table before frying.

To make the wings, remove the top of the wing with kitchen scissors or a sharp knife. Open the wing top cover and cut off between the plate and the battery so that there are two parts.

Season the wings with flavored salt heat for approx 3 inches of oil in a large Dutch oven. If you are using an electric tabletop, charge the unit in the MAX range.

Heat the oil to 350 degrees Fahrenheit over medium-high

heat and check the temperature with an oven gauge. When the oil reaches 350 degrees, reduce the heat to medium low.

Carefully remove the wing in oil and approx. bake for 10 to 12 minutes until golden brown, then cook until the internal temperature reaches 165 degrees Fahrenheit.

Depending on the size of the pan, you may not dry all the wings at once. After preparing the wings, remove the wing from the plate coated with absorbent paper to dry off excess grease and allow the oil to return to 350 degrees before adding additional wings.

When all the wings are roasted, put them in a large bowl. Add 1/3 to 1/2 cup of sauce and remove the wings with the tabs until they are tightly closed. If the sauce is left, keep it in the refrigerator, covered, for up to a week.

Serve the wings immediately as the sauce soaks the layers.

The best script recipe

Macaroni and cheese determine food comfort. It's cream and cheese and every bite makes us a little happier than before we leave.

Son bread and cheese have been our favorite versions for a long time and we think it is impossible to repeat it at home. It is no better than swimming in a tasty pasta with a rich and slightly gloved sauce. If you combine them all, you will get the best cheese. It is difficult to maintain self-control, you just have to command a little; we order department stores and send a restaurant home, but we are sure to eat them all at once!

The problem is that the cheese is not as fresh as you might think. They use pure ingredients and their food is free of artificial colors, preservatives, sweeteners and other artificial flavors. The lock activates and locks in each store.

This is not surprising, especially in light of today's report, which serves over 3 million doses per month. But let's ask if the recipe for fresh grated cheese can rival the original. How did it all come together? Spoiler Warning: we love it. As a bonus, our recipe takes only 30 minutes from start to finish.

Gather the ingredients for the cheese recipe

When we look at the official list of raw materials, we try not to intimidate. There are a lot of ingredients on this list, but most are preservatives that should not be used at home. In terms of ingredients, the list is very simple.

The cheese sauce begins with flour and roux butter, which thickens the milk and cream. The sauce also contains cheddar cheese. The list of ingredients does not know the type of cheddar, but we know that the product description and the color of the finished food must be white cheddar.

We know that onions and garlic are not on the hard drive because the U.S. Food and Drug Administration (FDA) require food manufacturers to list these special ingredients. They demanded that no one list the "spices" used for packaging, so we had to figure it out.

After tasting the bowl, we were pretty sure of the strong taste and the cheese from the mustard, so we added a teaspoon of

Dijon mustard to the mixture. The spicy chocolate mustard gives too much heat and the mustard powder is too light, but Dijon seems to be doing the trick well.

You will find a complete list of ingredients, including step-by-step cooking instructions.

Good quality white cheddar is very important for copying cheese

The ingredients and cheese are fairly simple, but the luxury is treated with good quality cheddar cheese. Cabot Vermont white cheddar is a good choice if you find it because they say Vermont cheddar is used. Vermont cheddar is not found in the grocery store, so we chose Teddamook cheddar in Oregon. It will be delicious no matter which beach you choose, but don't forget to buy the best quality available in the store. We also want to warn you not to choose the packaging cheese for this recipe. Grated cheese is one of these foods that contain ingredients that you may not want to know. Manufacturers use cellulose (which is just a clever word for resin) to prevent cheese from accumulating in bags. This is a useless filler and the cheese will become more solid if you rub it on its own.

Don't worry if you don't find the right dough for this cheese copy recipe

Uniquely shaped dough on cheese, called a pipette. This dough has the shape of a short curved tube and each part has balls on the outside to help with a thick sauce like cheese sauce. The bad news is that you try it as soon as you don't get this pasta in your grocery store (even Barilla). The good news? It's fantastic, even if we use a module called Cellentani.

This means you can have fun and use your favorite pasta. Look for the dough with the outer edges creating small grooves that adhere to the sauce. It is best to use the dough with a hole or a crust to maximize the sauce that is obtained with each bite.

Don't hesitate to use your favorite mussels, corkscrews or ordinary macaroni. If you wish, you can switch to gluten-free dough, but keep in mind that the sauce is made with flour. Do not worry; we recommend replacing the cheese sauce to make this recipe completely gluten-free.

Cook the mixture according to the cheese recipe

This is the easiest part to create your recipe for a copy of a case, but you still have to plan ahead.

It always seems to require boiling water, especially when we're hungry; therefore, the vessel is usually covered with a lid to block the steam. According to the Cook Production Fund, the pot are not much faster than the dishes on display and only saves a few minutes. But we took extra time, especially considering that the pan cover meant we couldn't look at the water while it was warming up. This makes the process faster and faster!

When the water is boiling, add large amounts of salt. Season with salt, add a little salt to the preparation, so don't skip this step. From here, add the dough and bring to the boil for the time period specified on the package. For most pasta, it is 8-10 minutes. However, do not temporarily trust blind people; If time passes, enjoy the dough to make sure it is tasty enough. If consumed with cheese sauce, cook for a while so that it is a little complicated, but you don't want it to taste like it.

When you are satisfied with the elasticity, drain the dough on the roof, removing any excess water that may be frying the sauce. Set aside until you make a cheese sauce.

Until then, make buckwheat from a cheese making recipe

Once the pasta is cooked through, it's time to start the sauce. The cheese is based on a mixture of buckwheat, butter and flour, which makes a thick and soft sauce. Unfortunately, you can't leave the flour if you want a gluten-free sauce; the cheese is separated from the starch-free milk, giving it an oily and unpleasant texture.

Fortunately, you can still delete these foods by removing this step and starting with the next step, where you heat the milk and cream. When the hot milk and cheese melt, mix three tablespoons of corn with three tablespoons of water. Add the dilution to the cheese sauce and cook for a few minutes until the mixture is smooth and thick.

If you're not worried about making a gluten-free recipe, start and start your story. Melt the butter in a large skillet over medium heat until soft. Add the flour, roast continuously so that no raw pieces of flour are collected. Cook the mixture for 3-4 minutes, stirring constantly, until the flavor of the raw flour disappears. You can also find out when it happens when the mixture swells and becomes rich and fragrant.

Prepare the cheese sauce for the cheese recipe

When the roux is complete, it's time to squeeze the sauce. First, slowly add milk and cream to the pan. You will notice that the bag starts to take off as soon as you add cold liquid, but don't worry; During grinding, relax thick lumps and mix milk perfectly. Once all the milk has been added, mix the Dijon mustard and simmer. Continue to cook until the liquid becomes beautiful and thick, all around. It takes 10 minutes.

From now on, it is very important to remove the sauce from the heat before adding the cheese. If you throw the cheese into a mixer on the stove, the heat can damage the cheese, separate the oil from the cheese and turn the sauce into a liquid mess. Nobody wants it! Instead, remove the cheese very slowly from the heat, just add a little. Once the first punch is completely dissolved, add the other and stir constantly as you continue. When all the cheese is mixed, add salt and pepper.

Add the butter to complete this ricotta cheese recipe

It's time to get together. Once you have done this in advance, you can cool the cheese sauce in the fridge and reheat it when you are ready to serve. When you are ready for dinner, you can collect your dishes in minutes. Add the cooked mixture to the cheese sauce and stir until the whole mixture is well dressed. Sometimes the dough becomes very cold when we make the cheese sauce, but that's fine. Simmer the mixture over medium-low heat until everything is hot. If the sauce is too thick, you can add a little milk or cream to the dilution. Or, if the sauce looks too runny, cook the mixture for a few minutes to thicken the starch in the mixture.

This recipe serves as six types of ornaments, or approx. As four main courses, so you can save the rest. This cheese recipe is very hot, so don't spend more. Put in a bowl and leave to cool, not closed, in the refrigerator. Then cover the container with a lid and it will be safe to use for 3-5 days. When ready to heat, add 1/2 cup milk to the remaining pasta to melt the sauce.

Turn the cheese recipe into a main course

This milk recipe is a great decoration for grilled ribs, pork sandwiches, or even for festivals like Thanksgiving or Christmas. However, you can easily use it to prepare for the main course.

Mainly add cheese to a more complete meal by adding protein such as minced meat, chicken buffalo sauce or bacon. You can also add some vegetables to the cheese; Our favorites are broccoli, but dried cabbage, Brussels sprouts or bags of mixed vegetables can also be used.

If you want a smooth cheese, keep it as it is and arrange what's left. You can prepare side dishes, try fried vegetables or make a side salad stuffed with beans, cheese and tasty sauces.

This is as hot as pairing with a thin brush, so think bravely outside the box when making decorations.

What we like most is its soft texture and savory flavor, and our version surpasses both of them.

Dijon mustari is necessary to obtain a thin moisturizing form which prevents the cheese sauce from becoming too rich (although still very slow). In our version, there is certainly the right amount of cheese sauce for the pasta ratio. Not only does the sauce adapt to the dough, but it also collects the dough in a bowl and provides a good, rich and soft spoon for each piece.

One of the parts he took us to was the shape of the dough. Since we have not been able to do the shopping in the right way, companies don't seem right. Fortunately, the choice of a paste does not affect the aroma at all. He still eats like a tasty meal and now we know we don't have to go to town when we need good food.

The rest of the food is just as good, if not better, than the dough on the first day, so you can make the next double batch.

- A recipe for copying cheese
- Preparation time: 10 minutes
- Cooking time: 20 minutes
- Prepare: 4 portions as main course or 6 portions as a side dish

Ingredients:

- The shape is like a 1 kg crust or a straight top
- 1/4 cup of butter
- 1/4 cup whole wheat flour

- 2 cups of whole milk
- 1 cup of thick cream
- 2-1 / 2 cups of chopped white cheddar cheese
- 1 teaspoon of Dijon mustard
- 3/4 teaspoon halal salt
- 1/2 teaspoon black pepper

Direction:

Cook the mixture in salted water in a large reserve according to the instructions on the package. Tie well and set aside.

Meanwhile, in a large pan, melt the butter over medium heat until it becomes champagne and all around. It does not melt for 2 minutes.

Add the flour and continue stirring, cooking until the onions are soft and fragrant, all around. 3-5 minutes.

Gently pour in the milk and thick cream. Add the Dijon mustard and bring to a boil over medium heat. Cook for 10 minutes until the liquid dissolves.

Remove from the pan and add a handful of white cheddar cheese, stirring until it melts, before adding another handful of cheese. When all the cheese is added, add salt and pepper.

Add the cooked dough to the cheese sauce and mix. If the mixture cools while waiting for the cheese sauce, cook over low heat until it is hot.

If the cheese sauce is too thick, dilute it with drops of milk. Otherwise, if the sauce is too thin, gently cook the dough until it reaches the desired thickness.

Serve immediately. If left, add 1/2 cup of milk and heat the residue to soften the sauce.

The best recipe for broccoli with chipper soup

Nothing rises from the inside like an excellent bowl. Very herbs or chili bowls are perfect for dealing with the cold on a winter day, but other types of soup are available at any time of the year. Cream and cheese soup is a unique food resource; they taste rich and give you a warm and relaxed atmosphere when you are having a bad day. Incidentally, the broccoli soup with cheddar bread marks all the boxes and will become something you like the culprit.

We can love it so much that we make special efforts to discover that our soup is 100% made of pure ingredients and without preservatives. But they're not as fresh as you might think. Sure, they taste creamy and tasty, but former employees have found the soup as frozen "giant bricks". So we thought we could take the risk and see if we could make our favorite soup at home with a copy. How do we start? All in all, we can say that it is really fantastic!

I got the ingredients for the broccoli and chocolate soup

It's great to see the detailed list of ingredients in Bucolic cheddar cheese soup broccoli. It contains over 20 elements and some have a strange or exotic sound. It is extraction, potato starch, pasteurized cedar cheese, what is transformed into "food"? Do not be afraid; If you want to make soup at home, forget more than half of these ingredients and make it easier. Prepare with butter, flour, half and half, chicken, onions, carrots, broccoli and cedar cheese, nutmeg, salt and pepper, with accurate and detailed measurements.

If you look at your calories, you can divide the milk into two and a half, but the soup will not be so thick and dense. We also recommend using a homemade chicken set to prepare the richest and most fragrant soup. You can prepare it and store it in the refrigerator or store it on an underground shelf with a stove. However, since we know that most of us don't have time to sell stocks, you can also pick up quality boxes from the supermarket.

Can you prepare a gluten-free version of broccoli from Cheddar broccoli soup?

Most cream soups and cheese sauces contain flour, which eliminates those who follow a gluten-free diet. Can you just drop the oats and expect the best? We do not recommend American science says that a thick and soft sauce (like a cheese sauce) is made with saturated juice. The best way to suspend is to thicken the liquid. Because wheat is starch, so to speak add a handful of grated cheese immediately

Here we are, the moment of truth: it is time to make this soup out loud. If you add flour to the second step of wheat production, this extra cheese will be very painless. It is recommended to slow down when making gluten-free chocolate soup or if there is a risk that it will "spoil" the soup (where oil and fat are separated from the rest of the sauce). This can also happen if plain milk has been replaced with one and a half.

The best way to make soup creamier is to remove the soup

43

from the heat. At this point, everything is ripe, so there is no reason to stop the source. It also helps to shred the cheese at room temperature because it has the advantage of achieving melting temperature. Then add a small piece of grated cheese at a time and gently place each serving. When the cheese is completely melted and you no longer see the string floating in the soup, add the next punch. This gentle process ensures that the cheese is perfectly distributed in the soup, creating a warm and soft mixture.

Fill half of the Cheddar Broccolis cheese soup to prepare it

Some people like soft soup and others like thick soup, so you have more choices for this action. We thought our broccoli and cheddar soup was close to the original, but something was missing. It wasn't as thick as a soup restaurant, and their mouths were different. The whole soup is mixed in a high-performance Vitamin blender, but that made a little broccoli.

If we mix and mix half the soup in half, it's perfect. The soup has a cream for the body and the aroma of broccoli, but there are still soft grains that melt all their broccoli flour in the mouth. So let's leave you at this stage. If you want to taste your soup directly, shake it in half. If the main goal is not to combine the original soup, do not hesitate to mix as much or as much as you want.

How much broccoli and cheddar soup do we get?

I was very impressed by the comparison. Once you discover the benefits of cleaning half of the soup, the broccoli version of Broccoli Cheddar is the same as the original version. It was creamy broccoli, rich and perfectly cooked. Caramelized onion gives only candy and cheddar is bold and decadent. If you make this soup for a group of strong bread lovers, you may be wondering if you have consumed it.

For a truly authentic experience, serve this soup in a bowl of bread. We use natural melted squash, but you can take out dry bread and chew it inside. It doesn't even serve soup in a bowl made with bread. The side of a baguette with fresh slices or soft Italian bread works well, especially if a slice holds for the last soup snack. This cheese soup is so good that you want to eat it until the last bite!

Recipe and instructions for broccoli broth Cheddar

Preparation time: 10 minutes

Cooking time: 40 minutes

4 parts

Ingredients:

- 1/4 cup plus 1 tablespoon butter, separate
- 1 medium yellow onion, cut
- Flour 1/4 cup
- 2 half cups *
- 2 cups chicken
- 1/2 pound of fresh broccoli in about 3 cups chopped
- Carrots 1 cup, glaze match
- 8 ounces of minced cedar cheese, about 2 cups

- 1/4 teaspoon minced walnuts
- Halal salt and black pepper to taste
- If you fail half and half, use 1 cup of heavy whipped cream and 1 glass of pure milk

Indications:

In a large saucepan (2 liters), melt 1 tablespoon butter at medium high heat. Add the chopped onion and cook for 5 minutes, stirring occasionally, until the onion is golden and tender. Remove the onions from the pan and set aside.

Put the dish back on the stove; clean it with the onion leftovers. Add 1/4 cup remaining butter. Cook over medium heat until butter is melted and melted, approx. 2 minutes.

Add flour and cook, stirring constantly, until the foam melts and no longer tastes like raw flour, approx. 3-5 minutes.

Gently shake half of the chicken. Bring the mixture to a boil over low heat and cook for 20 minutes until the liquid thickens slightly.

Put the onion back in the pan, along with the broccoli and carrots. Allow to cook over medium heat The best Chinese food recipes for home cooking

Chinese mix is often a wake-up call when we need something quickly, we must be happy for the whole family and when we just have to feed on the product. But while Chinese food, produced by restaurants, may look healthy because a lot of food is fried in vegetables, there is often fat, calories, and lots of hidden sodium. The good thing is it's easy to prepare homemade Chinese food; after learning one or two methods and sharing compartments with the most important things, it won't be interesting to touch your favorites from the hosting menu.

Soup

A bowl of hot soup is a great way to start Chinese food. Recipes can vary from basic to slightly complicated, but even the simplest are fun and enchanting. For example, egg drop soup only has three ingredients: soup, egg, and pepper and is made in several steps. Dumpling soup, on the other hand, requires more time and ingredients; as long as you get used to it, you just need to boil the soup with a little green onion. If you are a fan of spices, try hot and sour soup, including interesting ingredients such as black mushrooms or lilies.

Foreword and Dim Sum

There is no Chinese food that will be complete with delicious appetizers (called put-put foods) in varying amounts which are boring. It's easy to make a Chinese substitute for hosing sauce; when the sauce is mixed, all you have to do is pour the ribs and cook. Make salad dressing a little easier, which can be prepared quickly, the rest of the cooked chicken can be used well and is flexible enough to suit different tastes. Spring rolls are always a popular product, filled with pork and vegetables, freshly roasted and fried. If you want to try it with edible deer, flower dishes are a good choice because they don't need to cook meat first.

Beef

The Chinese restaurant menu always offers a large selection

of meat dishes, often accompanied by rich vegetables and sauces. Almost every Chinese restaurant menu contains beef broccoli, where grilled meat is marinated in a mixture of soy sauce, rice wine, oatmeal and sugar, then cooked with cooked broccoli. Add the potato flour and water mixture to the sauce mixture. Beef paprika and black bean sauce contain ingredients that are indispensable in Chinese cuisine, fermented black beans which have a strong taste and blend with garlic and chili. A typical element of the Chinese menu is roast beef with seafood sauce, because seafood sauce enhances the taste of meat.

Pork dish

Pork is the most popular meat in China. The Chinese can prepare a handful of very delicious food, including moo shun pork, using a little pork; Marinated pork is fried in vegetables and spices, served with thin pancakes and tubing sauce. If your sweet dishes are more your business, try sweet and sour pork with pineapple, which is prepared in Cantonese style to be cooked. To make a special dish, place a lion's ax, which is a popular dish for Chinese celebrations.

Chicken dish

The Chinese believe that they use every part of the chicken, including the legs, but this recipe only requires bird white meat. My favorite, but often secret, reason is General Tao's chicken, but when it is made in a chicken coop, there is no need to cook it in depth; instead, you can lightly fry it before throwing it with aromatic sauce. Moo Goo Gail's pan basically means it's chicken with mushrooms, and that's this dish, mixed with delicious sauce. For a little spasm, try chopped chicken because the chicken pieces are fried in vegetables, beans and salsa.

Seafood

Shrimp and lobsters, clams, and other fish occupy a prominent place on the Chinese food menu. Popular Sacheduan dishes include Kung pal shrimp, which contains spicy tongue from chili, cheese and ginger in a light sauce. Shrimp filled with honey seeds are rather soft, sweet to the touch and offer dishes that are slightly different from typical dishes. If you feel a little adventurous, you can try Cantònese lobster, where the lobster tail is quickly fried and served with fermented black beans and pork sauce.
Pasta dish

Chinese noodles are served from children to adults

Chicken Copycat Chipotle

We love good script recipes and that's okay. The adobe carpet and sauce give us the authentic Chipotle flavor we need.

MATERIAL

- 1/2 red onion, almost chopped
- 2 cloves garlic
- 1 chili pepper in adobo's sauce, plus 2 tbsp. dressing
- 3 tablespoons, vegetable oil
- 1 tbsp. dried oregano
- 1/2 tablespoon qimnon ready
- Halal salt

- Fresh ground black pepper
- 1 pound of chicken breast without basket
- NOT BASKETBALL
- Rice
- Maize
- Black beans
- Guacamole
- Dressing
- Slices of lime

INSTRUCTIONS

Mix the onion, garlic, chili pepper and adobo's sauce, oil, oregano and cumin together with the food preparation until cooked through season with salt and pepper. Put the spices and chicken in a large disposable plastic bag and massage all over the body to coat the chicken. Leave to soak in the fridge for at least 2 hours.

Bring the chicken to room temperature and heat over high grill. Cook until cooked through, 8 minutes on one side.

Serve the chicken in rice with the desired sauce.

How your kids love Filipino food

It can be difficult to have children: let them choose food and take out the trash, give them healthy food and never touch it. If you are a parent, you may be familiar with the anger that comes with each meal. But it doesn't have to be this way, especially if you know your Philippine food. Our disc is healthy and tastes natural, so it is

Your kids will surely love it.

If they are too dizzying, you can always change the old Philippine food recipes to their taste. Sometimes the extra variations of spices or presentations will suffice. Still confused? Here are some things you can do to make your kids love Philippine cuisine, as well as some recipes you should try.

Plan your meal together

Invite your children to help you with weekly meals. You can choose dinner once a day and have them decide on the rest of the week. To help them make healthy choices, let them choose Philippine recipes from cookbooks. The thing is, they feel connected. If they know they are helping to combine food, they will be more open to your idea.

When planning your meal, make sure you maintain the right balance between your desires and your child's. Don't plan meat the next day after choosing pork or frying. Since the point is to give them control, try not to limit them to your choice. Let them choose first and then add to your favorites to match them.

According to their taste

Get instruction from your child's junk food. Do you always choose biscuits and sweets or do you like delicious potatoes and biscuits? If they have a sweet tooth (most kids have it), sit down at your old recipe or serve sweet just like token for breakfast or snack in the evening. If they like a little spice, add chili to your soup or season them to taste.

Some children change their choices, which can be a little

harder. If your child likes sweets and cooks the next day, make salsa and salsa. So when you don't like food, they can always take their favorite sauce and turn it into something you like. This is a fast food that fits easily for all children.

Grilled meat

Ingredients:

- ½ kg sausage, minced meat
- ½ kg minced beef
- 1 c slice of bread
- 2 teaspoons curry powder
- 2 onions, chopped
- 1 egg
- Milk ½ c
- 1 c of water
- Salt, pepper and parsley
- Dressing:
- ¼ c Worcestershire sauce
- ½ c tomato sauces
- 2 teaspoons vinegar
- 2 tablespoons lemon juice
- 1 teaspoon of coffee powder
- . Butter
- Packaged powdered sugar 1 / c

Method:

Mix in a bowl of beef, sausage, bread crumbs, curry powder, onion, salt, pepper and parsley. Fry the eggs gently and add to the mixture. Add water and milk and mix well. Knead the pan or skillet, then toss in the meat mixture cook over medium heat for about 30 minutes or until meat is cooked through. Mix all the ingredients together in the sauce and bring to a boil until thickened, pour over half-baked bread, cook and cook for 45 minutes for occasional drinking.

Be creative

Promotions often differentiate between foods that children love and those that don't. Make your food more delicious by decorating your favorite food like slices of cheese or sausage. You can also have them design their own decorations. Look for Philippine recipes that may contain multicolored ingredients, i.e.

How to make pineapple stuffed chicken breast

What I like about this recipe is that it is easy to prepare with ready-made ingredients. It takes an hour to cook, but it will be nice to wait. This recipe will do 4 good services.

Tip: if you don't have chopped pineapple, you can use table or rings ... just use a potato masher or food processor to squeeze them.

Pineapple-stuffed chicken breast

- 2/3 cup hot water
- 2 tablespoons butter or margarine
- Mix of 2 cups full of boxes, chicken aroma
- 8 pineapples can be mashed with syrup
- 4 skinless, skinless halved chicken breasts
- 1/2 green pepper, chopped
- 1/2 chopped red pepper

53

- 2 tablespoons brown sugar
- 2 spoons of white vinegar
- 1/4 teaspoon chopped ginger
- Preheat the oven to 350 degrees.

Stir in hot water and butter in a large bowl until the butter melts. Stir in 2 cups of chicken filling until it is dressed and begins to soften. Mix the chopped green and red peppers and half of the pineapple and syrup.

Spread the filling mixture evenly over the chicken and roll it up firmly. Secure yourself with a toothpick. Place in a pan with the rest remaining in the center of the pan.

In a small bowl, combine the rest of the pineapple with the syrup, icing sugar, vinegar and ground ginger. Spread this sauce over the chicken. Place the pan in the preheated oven, set it at 350 degrees for 50 to 60 minutes or until it is cooked.

How to make an easy chicken recipe

Got an easy-to-kill chicken recipe for testing? Start by reviewing your recipe to see if any ingredients are needed. If there are seven or more ingredients, it is generally not recommended if you are looking for a simple and easy chicken recipe. This guarantees your success and in the end the dish will taste good. For example, an unbroken chicken dish with white wine should be created: chicken breast, fermented mushrooms, butter, flour, onion, chicken broth and white wine.

Since finding unusual items can take a long time, choose a recipe that is not a problem. You should use the ingredients found in the supermarket or grocery store. We also recommend using the ingredients used previously.

Decide before you buy if you want to use whole chicken or chicken pieces. Although the whole chicken is flavored, the chicken pieces have a much faster cooking time. So, if you're concerned about the weather, choose skinless breasts or tender chicken. Fresh, unfrozen chicken is much faster and safer to cook than when you have the most active chicken offerings. However, it is best to use the type of chicken shown in your recipe.

Once the recipe is in place and make sure you don't miss anything, go to the store to collect all your ingredients. Put the ingredients that go into your recipe on the kitchen table with all the tools you need to cook.

If you need to cut or some other preparation, does it first, keep the chicken away from other items to prepare? Always wash all areas of the detergent after putting the raw chicken in contact with any surface. The cutting board can be cleaned with a bleach solution or put in the dishwasher.

Use the right saucepan or frying pan to prepare your chicken. Often the recipes will show you which pots, pans, or pans to use, otherwise you can use whatever you have on hand. A good pan for chicken is a must for most recipes.

When will dinner be ready? To know when dinner is over, you should allow about half an hour to prepare and up to an hour to cook your chicken dish. The purchase time is not included. When you try different chicken recipes, you will find simple chicken recipes.

How to make super thin sandwiches for the perfect paint

I'm talking about how I skip the empty calorie picnic and continue to have delicious and fun picnics. Have you had a child picnic? If not, can you imagine? The trip to the village, the garden or the grass is gone. It could be a garden. Be there, accompanied by your best friends and family; and here is what you should bring with you:

What the list should include in a good picnic

Food: a picnic means an outdoor meal and therefore also the event / occasion and the food eaten. A good picnic should be tasty, healthy, and fun to eat and varied.

Cooking Tips - How To Make Vegetable Soup And Rice Soup

According to some chefs, the food that Rachael Ray's cooking is very tasty. No wonder most moms in the US only choose brands that have given themselves name in terms of quality of food. Rachael Ray's kitchenware is not only reliable but also elegantly designed to brighten up any kitchen table.

Ingredients in vegetable soup:

- The fourth bottle is 60 ml of butter.
- 1 cup of celery with 250 ml
- 1 cup of 250 ml chopped carrots
- 1 cup of potatoes with 250 ml
- Half cup cups weighing 125 ml
- Glass of chopped onions 60 ml

- 1/4 cup thinly cut 60 ml
- 1 cup of boiling water, 250 ml
- 2 teaspoons of 10 ml of salt
- 1/2 tsp 2 ml pepper
- 1 teaspoon of sugar 5 ml
- 1 cup of frozen 250 ml beans
- 1 cup of 250 ml chopped green pepper
- 4 cups of 1l fried milk
- 1/4 cup chopped parsley 60 ml
- 1/2 cup 125 ml hard chopped cheddar cheese

Procedure:

First, the butter has to be melted in the large pan of Rachael Ray. Then add celery, carrots, potatoes, turnips, onions, oak, water, salt, pepper and sugar. Then cover and cook on low heat until the vegetables are soft and fresh. Boil on low heat for about 10 minutes. Then add the beans and green peppers; cook again for five minutes or until all the vegetables is tender. Then add hot milk. Then sprinkle with parsley. And finally, pour it into the soup bowl and sprinkle grated cheese over.

Raw Soup Range:

- 2 tbsp of 30 ml of butter
- 2 tablespoons of 30 ml water
- Cut half a glass of green beans into 125 ml diagonally
- 2 medium carrots, 2 medium thin slices
- 2 cups of beaks in 500 ml thin strip
- 2 beers, thin pepper (white only) 2

- Half a cup of 125ml chopped celery
- Half a cup of water, 125 ml
- Half a cup of 125ml fresh or frozen beans
- 2 cups, chopped kale, 500 ml
- 1 tbsp of 7 ml salt
- Four teaspoons pepper 1 ml
- One teaspoon of pepper 2 ml
- 4 cups of milk 1l
- Half a cup of 125ml jam
- 2 teaspoons of 10 ml of fresh fennel

Procedure:

First, heat the butter in a large Rachael Ray pan. Then add two tablespoons (30 ml) of water and beans. Then cover and cook over high heat for about 3 minutes. Shake pan often. Then add carrots, turnips, chives, celery and half a glass (125 ml) of water. Then cover and cook for seven minutes or until the vegetables are almost tender. Then add the peas and simmer for about five minutes. Then add the cabbage, salt, pepper, pepper and milk. Boil for five minutes. Add the salad and heat on the pan. And finally, pour the soup into a bowl and sprinkle fennel over.

How to prepare lobster for lobster recipe

Caravanserai is an excellent crust, not to mention the most expensive. The cost of lobsters is for good reason. Caravanserai is planted or sold only after it has crossed a certain weight limit. Sounds easy, but did you know that lobsters take a year to gain pounds? It takes seven years to grow seven pounds of greasy lobster on your hard drive.

Surely something that takes so long to grow is liquid and delicious. In this case, the lobster does not disappoint. However, improper cooking will spoil the taste of lobsters. It is therefore necessary to carefully follow the lobster recipe to maintain good taste.

These dripping shellfish are usually cooked in three ways:

boiling, steaming and roasting. We discussed how adrenaline in lobster changes the taste of meat, but it's still proven. However, to be sure, some suggest hypnosis lobsters before boiling to avoid adrenaline. To mesmerize this adorable crustacean, simply rub or rub your head or stomach. You will see that their tails will fall off and that their clothes will be thinner. Take advantage of this moment and add it to a large pot of boiled salted water. To do this, first place a jar of hot water. Remove when the color turns reddish orange. Serve immediately with fresh or chilled butter and remove the meat according to your favorite lobster recipe.

Another method of cooking lobsters is steaming. Since this method uses only steam heat, the lobsters remain spilled even when they are fully cooked because the delicious liquid is not lost in the water. Since lobsters do not drown in juice, they must taste good. Kill the lobster before stealing to prevent the crabs from coming out of the pot. You can pour it in hot water or freeze it. Take a large skillet and a large grill to place the lobster. It is best to steam the shellfish just to avoid crowds. Season the boiled juice with salt, pepper and herb and bring to a boil. Add the lobster and steam. Make sure the liquid does not reach the shelf or that your shells are boiling instead of steam. As always, get rid of all shrimp when they are red to avoid overeating.

If you are brave enough to kill lobsters, you can rinse them as well. This is a way to avoid slowing down the heart. Remove the knife and place it in the center of the crust. Rub the scalp to quickly remove scratches. Slide the knife from head to tail to reveal the sweet meat. According to some lobster recipes, cut the meat, mix it with other ingredients and refill the mixture in the empty lobster shell. Cut them on paper and grill for a few minutes. Other recipes say you can give the meat a good Italian cheese crust and let it down in the oven until the cheese has melted. Enjoy!

How to make lobster and make peanut butter? New method in England

Learn that you don't have to be scary about choosing a lobster dinner. It is very easy if you follow these simple guidelines. In order to make the lobster dinner much better, I recommend the New England cooking method.

Maine Classic Lobster Tip:

1. Fill a pan with water.

2. Add 1/8 cup of sea salt.

3. Turn on the stove and bring the water to a boil.

4. As soon as the water boils quickly, add the lobster to the pan, making sure that they are primarily submerged.

5. Cover the pan so that it boils quickly.

6. As soon as the water boils again, turn the burner to a medium height to boil more slowly and do not allow the water to boil.

7. Cook the lobster for 10 minutes for the first needle and for another 3 minutes for each additional pound of lobster, for example, a two-pound lobster for 13 minutes.

8. When the lobster turns completely red, it takes off.

9. Serve with peanut butter and enjoy!

Take out the butter recipe
1. Melt the butter in a pan with a small to medium skillet and slowly bring the butter up

Bring to a slow boil.
2. Remove the foam and solids that have accumulated on the surface of the butter.

3. Remove from the heat and gently lubricate the extracted butter in small measuring cups.

Karavidha is not just about eating, but a unique sugar beet that offers fun, adventure and joy to many people who share the extraordinary experiences the caravan offers.

How to cook lobster
How to make the perfect pizza: a professional chef offers detailed tips and instructions Here are some tips and tricks to make your pizza perfect.

Use a pizza stone, brick, pizza oven or terracotta dish to bake pizza. Don't expect pizza pans, non-stick trays and "normal" bread ovens.

If you cut your pizza into bricks, terracotta or warm stone about 240 ° C or 470 ° F, you get an excellent structure and fresh base

Make a thin foundation. The dough should rise properly, be curved and stretched in a rolled or thin medium mode. Pizza should be a thin jump - not on a thick bread plate. Learn how to make the right pizza and then play it with a reference standard.

Do not add too much sauce, cheese or sauce. It looks generous and luxurious, but no. It loses its structure and the pizza base becomes wet and goes under the weight of all the wet, gorgeous peaks. Not good! This is the golden rule

Make your own dough. No matter how good or comfortable the Boboli bases and frozen pizza dough are, they will not be able to compete with the raw baked pizza dough from the beginning. It is easy to make your own dough. It can be even easier than traveling to the store.

Never bake pizza with sauce. Dry, very fresh and attractive. Roll out the dough with the sauce, cheese, cold cuts that way. Then fry it raw. Follow the steps in the section below.

Make or buy a sauce that tastes good. Pizza is so simple - so the quality of the ingredients succeeds - it's delicious and economical and allows the ingredients to work together. Delicious tomato sauce, high quality chopped mozzarella and no need for toppings either. That's it Then set the temperature and slide the pizza on a baking sheet and bow, perfect each time.

How to make pizza

Make the dough and let it rise to room temperature until it is twice as big.

Make pizza sauce with tomatoes or use the ones that are bought very tasty.

Preheat oven to 220-240 C (425-470 ° F).

Cut the raw material. They are thin slices.

Roll out the pizza dough over the floured bench 1/2 inch or 1/5 inch thick. Therefore, a small serum or nice cartridges help to break down Optional.

Make sure the pizza is powdered so as not to stick to it. If you don't have a pizza crust that you can slide down and lift up, wrap in baking paper.

Spread the tomato sauce over the pizza. Not too much sauce, but cover the base so that the sauce is about 1 cm or 1/2 inch around the outer edge. The amount of pizza sauce should be less than half the weight of the dough. 80-90 g of tomato sauce is used for 220 g of pasta.

Cover with very lightly chopped mozzarella cheeses. Use only 70-80 g of cheese for 220 g of pizza dough (about 1/3 of the weight of the dough)

Sprinkle gently on the pizza cutting the memory in half, so it doesn't tear when you run and get up.

The spread should be about half the low volume of the dough. Pre-cook raw water that loses water moistens and moisturizes pizza.

Throw the pizza on the hot pizza stone or directly on the floor in the hot oven.

Cook approximately. 7 minutes. The pizza side should be the edge. The pizza base should be brown and fresh. The pizza head should be bubbling and delicious.

Remove from the oven, then slice and eat or serve.

Here are three pizza dough recipes.

We use sour cucumbers, the other two for convenience if sour cucumbers are not easily made. All three taste delicious and work every time.

Enjoy new and improved pizzas.

The basis of wheat and rye pizzas

- Flour, bread (high protein) 1000g
- Rye flour - 200g dark
- Acute (daily dose) 200g
- Salt 30g
- Water 600 g
- Yeast, immediate, dry, powder 2 g
- Mix with the dough hook in the mixer. Six minutes slow and medium speed 1 minute

- then rest for 10 minutes
- Then run for another 3 minutes
- then rest for 10 minutes and then run for 3 minutes.
- Degree 210-240 g. Cover with a damp glue or cloth and make (lift).
- 2nd recipe of pizza base
- Flour, bread (high protein) 1500 grams
- Wheat 150 grams
- Olive oil 75 grams
- Salt 20 grams
- Water 900 grams
- Yeast, dry, 2 grams (or 10 g fresh)
- Mix all the ingredients and cook for 10 minutes until elastic.
- Distribute 220 g of balls and create in a warm place without direct heat.
- 3rd pizza base recipe
- Yeast, volume, dried powder 7 g (35 g fresh yeast) 21 g / 105 g
- Water 190 g 570 g
- Love 20 g 60
- Flour, bread (high protein) 375 g 1125
- 5 g salt 15
- 100g 300 olive oil.

How to make better bread at home?

If you are a young baker, then you are in the right place! There are many ways to improve your bread, but this seems to be a secret health

Making healthy bread at home can be as simple as turning flour into whole wheat. The health benefits of whole grains are all the news today, and even if you don't like the smell of whole wheat bread, just replace it with a small portion, you still get health benefits without cutting it. This is also good advice for small families. They will never know that the bread you burn is better than stored bread or white bread. Only they will know this extraordinary taste!

Multiple extra tasks

If you are just starting to bake with a bread maker, you may notice that it is different from baking in a normal oven. Many bread manufacturers choose to use vitamin C, wheat gluten, from a combination of both to improve their structure and flavor. Hodgson Mills creates a great mix of these ingredients, suitable for beginners. They also make special flour of a quality that can be enjoyable to experience.

The inference

There are many ways to improve bread. Quality, food and perfumes can be adjusted to suit your needs. Playing with the percentage of content you use can yield great results. Don't change things too much, or you may be in trouble instead of his masterpiece. Adjust gradually, in one case, especially for salt and sugar. Changing teaspoons can produce significant results.

How to make glass donuts

This recipe shows you how to make glass donuts at home. We need three sets of ingredients: one for donuts, one for icing and one for chocolate coating.

Ingredients for donuts

- Top - three spoons
- Pure milk - glass (at 110 Fahrenheit)
- Flour - two and a half cups (excluding flour for repeated surfaces)
- Sugar - two teaspoons
- Salt - half a teaspoon
- Vanilla extract - one teaspoon
- Egg yolk - three, big
- Butter: four spoons at room temperature, not peeled
- Vegetable oil - ideal for frying
- Ingredients for frozen sugar
- Sugar candy - glasses and a half
- Milk - three or four teaspoons
- Vanilla extract - two teaspoons
- Ingredients for chocolate glaze
- Sugar candy - glasses and a half
- Cocoa powder - four tablespoons
- Milk - two tablespoons
- Vanilla extract - two teaspoons

How to make a shiny donut

Place two tablespoons of yeast in three-quarters of a cup of hot milk in a medium bowl. (We make donuts first, then chocolate for the donuts.)

Gently add three quarters of a cup of flour to the bowl and

stir until smooth. Cover the bowl and set aside for 30 minutes.

In a mixing bowl, take the remaining hot milk and mix with the remaining yeast. Then add the mixture obtained in step 2 to the bowl, with the sugar, vanilla extract, salt and egg yolk. Mix the "medium" setting until a soft and gentle mixture is obtained.

Add half a cup of flour to the mixture and turn on the blender for 30 seconds on low setting.

Then add the butter (at room temperature) and stir for about 30 to 40 seconds.

Turn off the blender and add the flour to the mixture. You need to add a quarter cup of flour to this frozen donut recipe at a time.

Between the additions of the fourth cup of flour, knead the dough with a dough hook on the mixer. Knee in middle position the dough should remove the skin from the side of the bowl and be soft and moist enough to roll. When you are satisfied with the consistency, cover the bowl and refrigerate for one hour. You can cool up to 12 hours.

The next step in the frozen donut recipe is to roll the dough over the surface of the flour dough for approx. It should be rolled to a thickness of half an inch. Cut out the shape of the donut with a donut or cookie cutter. When finished, roll up the waste mixture again and cut the donut shape again.

Set the donut aside and cover with plastic wrap. Usually, a

donut needs ten to 20 minutes to prove and double its size. Every few minutes, make sure the donuts are ready to cook. You can do this by taking the donut lightly - if the dough appears immediately, spend more time. If the mixture comes slowly, the donuts are ready to cook.

To check the donut, make a pan by adding two inches of oil and heat to 350 Fahrenheit. You can check the temperature with a thermometer.

Use a wooden stick or a metal spatula, lower the nuts several times with the oil and cook each side for about a minute. When the donut turns golden brown, remove it from the pan and set aside on the shelf.

Cook all the donuts at the same temperature. You have now learned how to make sparkling chocolate from the start!

Now make a chocolate coating for the donut. Add the sugar and cocoa powder to a bowl and mix the milk and vanilla well - slowly add little by little. The glaze should be poured, smooth.

When the frosting is finished, transfer to a shallow bowl and pour the donut. Place the scintillating nuts on a wire holder and let stand until the frosting melts.

This recipe makes the donut tender and tender from the start and the end result is very verbally delicious! If you know how to make shiny chocolate chips at home, you will never want to go back to the bakery again.

How to make Fondue Night the perfect social food?

An evening with family and friends can be a great addition to a busy lifestyle. Learning how to fondue will help you spend time with loved ones in the past. When do you enjoy great repentance with delicious food without spending a lot of money or slavery for hours in the kitchen? If you do not remember, it may be time to taste the fondue at home.

A fondue for all tastes

While "fondue" refers to a hot liquid that immerses you in a delicious treat, you can choose from several types of fondue. The most common funds are:

* Fondue cheese. The types of fondue can be wine, beer, kirsch, milk or cream and lots of cheese. Of course, spices are also added to make everything taste better. There are even Italian, Mexican or pizza versions of this delicious dish. The most common plungers are bread sticks, but cooked vegetables, cooked meat and apples also taste good.

* Chocolate fondue Chocolate fondue is a delicious treat at the end of the day. You can try different chocolates like milk, black or white milk and you can even mix several varieties. Again, milk, cream or alcoholic beverages are often added to improve texture and taste. The most common tumors in chocolate fondue are: fruits How to make the best donut?

If you want to create a delicious donut, you will need to follow a few steps to make sure you get the best one. For example, you need to prepare the right mixture, as this usually determines the final product. If you get the wrong mix, you will probably get the wrong donut, but if you get it you will enjoy the donuts.

You can try many donut recipes and you need to follow them strictly to get the perfect final product.

Once you have the right mix, find the right outfit that you will use to make sure you get a delicious donut. Be sure to use hot oil at about 370 degrees to properly prepare the donuts. Do not overload the dryer as this can lead to improper preparation. You need to do two or three dives at a time. Roll the donuts as they begin to rise. This ensures that both sides are cooked properly. They should not be overtaken and removed if they turn slightly golden.

When making the dough, be sure to use the softest dough available. You can use the fridge to make it more comfortable. Always use clean oils, as contaminated oils can change or even complicate your health. Once you're done, let it soak in the oven for a minute before removing completely. Place the oven on a paper towel to soak up all the oil. Never turn the donut over, but use it by lowering it to get the best results.

How to make healthy blue muffins?
Do blueberry muffins have weaknesses? I've loved them for as long as I can remember, but I don't really abuse them. Blueberries are healthy, but blueberries are not found in today's oven! These are great calories and sugars that my body doesn't like. Of course, they taste great, but within an hour or two, I was shocked and angry - I tried to avoid that

feeling.

Did you know that kibitz sold in cafes, supermarkets and vending machines today are twice as high as those sold in the 1960s as and more than three times the standard portion?

Blueberry muffins - nutritional status

Few online searches have shown that blueberry muffins sold at Starbucks contain 450 calories, 22 grams of fat and 31 grams of sugar, but the Dunkin Donuts derivative is even worse! This is more than twice the caloric value of frozen squash and more than typical chocolate croissants.

Here come the healthy blueberry muffins. There are various ways to increase blueberry kef food. Here are some of my favorite things.

How to make healthy blue muffins?

- Use whole wheat flour instead of white
- Reduce the amount of sugar used. I often cut the required sugar into muffins by 25-50%
- Reduce the amount of fat used. 1/4 cup butter or oil in one dose is usually enough.
- Add more blueberries
- Look for recipes that contain flaxseed, which is an excellent source of omega-3

For a realistic dose, bake in regular muffin boxes

Here is a recipe for examining blueberry muffins. Use whole grain flour combined with a moderate amount of sugar and butter, so it still tastes great, but the calories in typical coffee muffins are ready.

Whole blueberry muffins
Makes 12 muffins

- 4 tablespoons butter
- 1/2 cup sugar
- 2 large eggs
- 2 cups white pasta or whole wheat
- 2 tablespoons close
- 1/2 teaspoon salt
- 1/2 cup milk
- 2 tablespoons vanilla extract
- Almond extract 1/4 teaspoon
- 1 1/2 to 2 cups (about 1 cup) blueberries, fresh or frozen
- 1 tablespoon of sugar mixed with 1/2 teaspoon of cinnamon to be sprinkled on top (optional)
- Preheat the oven to 375 ° F. Grease 12 cups of muffins with non-stick vegetable soup.

Beat the butter and sugar in a large bowl with an electric mixer until light and creamy. Add eggs, one by one, beating well after each addition.

In another bowl, mix together the flour, baking powder and salt. Add the dry matter to the butter / sugar / egg mixture and whisk evenly.

How to make cinnamon rolls - simple recipe for lunch

Learn how to make cinnamon rolls with this simple brunch recipe!

Channel roll

Many people think you should spend all day making delicious cinnamon rolls perhaps. Many recipes are eventually arranged this way. But if you want to learn how to make cinnamon rolls, this simple brunch recipe is for you.

By the way, if you have trouble getting the kids out of bed in the morning, there is nothing for them to get off or get cold cinnamon drinks from the oven in the morning. The aroma of a single aromatic cinnamon is enough to awaken the sharpness of the animal.

Ingredients:

- 1 egg
- 3/4 c. milk
- 3 tsp. Bisques
- 2 tbsp. melted butter
- 2 tbsp. add channels
- 1/2 tsp. sugar
- 1/4 tsp. sugar Packets
- 2 tablespoons hot water

Procedure:

1. Preheat oven to 350 degrees.

2. Bring the eggs into the bowl and mix the Bisques and milk

until soft and hard.

3. Cook lightly until soft and smooth.

4. Scroll through a 10 × 8 inch rectangle.

5. Cover evenly with butter, then cinnamon and sugar.

6. Wrap the mixture tightly, starting with the wide side (10 inches). Cover the edge of the roller with a seal.

7. Place the wheels on an uncoated baking sheet with the tip down.

8. Cut roll 1 using scissors, almost cut to the end, but not enough.

9. Bake for 15 to 20 minutes.

10. Mix sugar and dessert water while cooking until ready. After cooking, the frosting is rolled with a mixture of frosting.

Tips:

If you've ever wanted to learn how to make cinnamon rolls [it's a simple lunch recipe! Not only simple and easy, but also versatile. If necessary, you can taste lemon juice by adding a teaspoon or a tablespoon. This adds an extra element of flavor without going overboard.

If you fly on busy weekends (and even weekends) and want something more extensive than delicious cinnamon spices, you may want to add wine, apples, pecans or even nuts to your recipe so you can get more snacks or you can have your food in a moment, not just the guilty pleasures that this bread has made in the morning. You can also sprinkle sugar-free chocolate snacks to add chocolate cake and delicious fat-free flavors without being overwhelmed.

Falafel with fried hummus and tabbouleh

If my message was written on the basis of a love for special food, this message would be too late. Since becoming vegan, falafel has become my favorite dish. Don't be fooled by me; I still like falafel, but I tend to mix it with chicken or peeled lamb, spanakopita or tits. Falafel is a variety of Mediterranean dishes that I like. However, since the adoption of the herbal diet, falafel has been given a new status. I think that's because falafel doesn't seem to have more veganism than the other foods available. When I try to find vegan options at restaurants, they often get insane and feel a lot of care. Nacho's orders at Baja Fresh Bar always give the staff a moment: "No meat, cheese, sour cream and guacamole. Thank you!" I usually have a plate of chips and beans if I'm lucky. But the falafel has become vegan! Likewise hummus! And pita bread! Yeah! So falafel became my own food group in my food life, so I realized I had to learn how to do it myself. Of course, falafel is not food in itself, so I made mine with homemade soils, pita bread with whole grains and a table salad. You can pack everything in oatmeal cookies for a nice mobile lunch the next day!

Toasted Falafel
- 15 oxide cans, emptied and rinsed
- Chopped onions

76

- 2 cloves minced garlic
- 2 teaspoons cumin
- Teaspoon coriander
- . A teaspoon of salt
- Cilantro Cilia Cup
- And a cup of parsley
- 2 tablespoons olive oil

Preheat oven to 400 ° C. Mix all ingredients; store a tablespoon of olive oil in a food processor. The process is up to the combination, but still thick, scraping the edges if necessary. Make 16 balls. Be careful about the report; if it is too small, it dries; outdoors it will not be too big and cool. Add a frying pan and the oil with the remaining olive oil Chef.

Ways to have a light breakfast

It can be very tempting to fry breakfast or eat a donut for breakfast, especially if you're in a hurry. There are better alternatives that are fast and healthy at best. One of the best options is to prepare a coarse breakfast. This vibration does not contain many ingredients and can easily be prepared with a mixer. This way you can have a light breakfast to start breakfast.

To get started, you'll need good results to have fun. Bananas are the best choice because they have a lot of food and therefore the cream will shake. Start by cutting the large banana and placing it in the blender. You can add a tablespoon of yogurt or peanut butter for extra flavor. Simple vanilla yogurt is a good choice, but you can also choose to use flavored yogurt to suit your personal tastes. Many people love the taste of strawberry yogurt, which enhances the flavor of bananas.

After you have added the selected fruits and sauces, you can add milk. For students on a diet, skimmed milk or skim milk can be added as an additional way to cut calories. Pure milk is also good to use. Make a cup of your favorite milk. Some people like to add extra milk to give it an extra flavor, and for those who love chocolate, you can always add chocolate syrup.

After you have obtained all the ingredients in the blender, you can disperse it and mix it in a smooth and desired consistency. This usually prepares two portions for breakfast, so it can always be extra to finish at lunchtime.

There are other ways to make breakfast smoothies healthier for extra nutrition. Many people would like to add some protein powder to soak up good proteins. Shaking protein is often more complete than just shaking. Another option is to add another banana fruit. Whatever type of fruit or recipe you use, this is the best way to start the day and a quick way to have breakfast.

How to make Hummus: tips and guidelines

If you want to learn hummus, there are many sources of information available as you start and get started. Such dishes are essential dishes in many countries in the Middle East. We must not forget that other global communities are gradually getting into the stomach. This allows for an online platform and its extensive resources, including recipe books, articles, blogs, books, videos and much more.

So learning is the easiest thing you can do now if you like to cook and try out new recipes and ideas. If you follow the correct guidelines, you will learn in a few minutes how to make hummus. To get started, you need to have the right ingredients in your food. Ingredients contain 1 to 16 ounces of chickpeas or chickpeas. You need 1/4 cup of liquid for a can of beans.

This requires 3-5 tablespoons of lemon juice, but it mostly depends on the general taste or maybe the taste you are trying to achieve. This dish cannot be prepared without 1 1/3 tablespoons of thin and 2 pieces of crushed garlic. 2 tablespoons of olive oil and 1/2 teaspoon of salt completes the essential ingredients. Other necessities you can consider for this dish include roasted red chili peppers, a variety of fried garlic recipes, spinach and feta. This variety determines the ingredients and extra quantity needed.

Preparation involves drying the beans and removing the liquid from the can. All ingredients must be placed in a blender or food processor with 1/4 cup of liquid beans added. Allow the mixing process for about 3-5 minutes on low speed to get a smooth and well-mixed paste. After this process, you can place the hummus in a serving bowl to form a shallow, shallow shape in the center of the dough. To learn how to make hummus, you also need to know that there are many ways in which you can enhance and enrich the taste of this food. You can add a lot of olive oil to the look The usual preparation time for the festival is 10 minutes. The main

ingredients in this special dish are 1 16 ounce chicken beans.
You can also replace them with dicks. You will need 1/4 cup
chicken beans. This requires 3-5 tablespoons of lemon juice
and the amount given here depends on the final taste
required. You will need 1 1/2 tbsp thin and about 2 crushed
garlic cloves. Other ingredients: 1/2 teaspoon salt and 2 tbsp
olive oil.

To make hummus, simply drain the chicken beans and
remove the liquid from the container. Follow the
combination of other ingredients available in the blender or
food processor. Then you need to add 1/4 cup of the liquid
to the chicken beans. The next thing is to stir for about 3-4
minutes at low heat until everything is mixed and smooth.
After mixing, place the dough in a bowl and create a base
dish in the center of the hummus.

Once you have made a shallow shape in the center of the
hummus, add a small amount of 1-2 tbsp of olive oil to the
well-formed solution. What you already get with parsley, but
not mandatory. Other service options include fresh toasted
and hot bread, which is served immediately. Then you can
cover and cool the ship. Other varieties include spicy holiday
with a red slice of chili. Other varieties can be produced by
the addition of cayenne pepper.

When it comes to hummus preparation you should also
know that the pot can be cooled for up to 3 days. It can be
stored in the freezer for a month. If you have stored the
hummus for too long, you may need to add olive oil to
combat the drought that occurs when the bowl cools. The art
is very popular in communities in the Middle East. However,

in communities in the Middle East, food is one of the children's favorites and is widely used as a beginner. There are many ways to produce hummus. The thing is to correct the methods and use the right ingredients in a good amount to get the hummus flavor.

How to Make Healthy Luggage Recipes

Starters are what serve people for the main meal. It can serve buffet-style recipes as well as other types of meetings and parties. There are many types of starter recipes: you can combine several ingredients to create the basic dish or you can spend time with a complex starter. Classic apps, including dishes such as shrimp cocktails, ventilation openings, hot dogs and many more. But these are not healthy options.

If you look at your numbers or want to make healthy decisions based on your initial recipes, you have many choices. What if I make a recipe for chicken soup or salad?

Start a buffet

If you offer a breakfast buffet instead of dinner, we recommend you make finger meals, but there are plenty of options too. You can make fresh fruit salad, vegetable rice salad, guacamole or vegetable crudity sauce and many more.

The sauce is chopped with sauce and made from homemade hummus or spicy Mexican sauce. Many recipes that are easy to sink can be created. Combine the mayonnaise with a mustard, curry or tomato sauce and make a tasty sauce. If you're adding tomato paste, you may want to add some

81

Worcestershire sauce to make Marie rose sauce (this is great for beginners to catch).

How to melt Turkey

This is a great example of how to make a delicious, tasty, tasty appetizer.

Ingredients:

10 slices of toast cut into 20 triangles

110 grams of measured fat less cheese

10 thin slices of turkey breast

Prepare:

Place half a slice of turkey on each toast triangle and place on the cheese. Cook by melting the turkey under the grill until the cheese has melted.

Put some currant sauce between the turkey and cheese if needed before grinding this recipe makes 20 cannabis. You can customize this recipe any way you like. Try using chicken breast instead of turkey or ham. You can use any cheese you like and try marinate instead of currant sauce or even a bit of piccalilli or spice. It starts hot and cold Turkish smelting is the best

ISBN 9798639702709